A chickaDEE Book

Text and Mish, Mash and Mush characters
© 2008 Owlkids Books Inc.

Spot illustrations © Remie Geoffroi

Publisher: Jennifer Canham
Associate Publisher: Angela Keenlyside
Editorial Director: Mary Beth Leatherdale
Editor: John Crossingham
Production Manager: Paul Markowski
Production Editor: Larissa Byj
Production Assistant: Kathy Ko

Art Direction and Design: Barb Kelly

We gratefully acknowledge the financial support of the Government of Canada through the
Book Publishing Industry Development Program (BPIDP) for our publishing activities.

 Conseil des Arts   Canada Council
du Canada   for the Arts

Library and Archives Canada Cataloguing in Publication

    The hilarious adventures of Mish and Mash : the story of how two
monsters--and you!--make the perfect joke book! / illustrated by Remie Geoffroi.

Summary: Collection of jokes, riddles, tongue twisters and brain teasers
    from chickaDEE Magazine.
ISBN 978-2-89579-208-6

    1. Wit and humor, Juvenile. 2. Riddles, Juvenile. 3. Puzzles--Juvenile
literature. I. Geoffroi, Remie II. chickaDEE Magazine

PN6371.5.H55 2008   jC818'.60208   C2008-903083-4

Printed and bound in Canada

Owlkids Publishing
10 Lower Spadina Ave., Suite 400
Toronto, ON M5V 2Z2
Ph: 416-340-2700
Fax: 416-340-9769

Owl kids

Publisher of

chirp   chickaDEE   OWL

www.owlkids.com

The Hilarious Adventures of Mish and Mash

The story of how two monsters - and _YOU_ - make the perfect joke book!

Illustrated by Remie Geoffroi

Owl kids

What's Inside

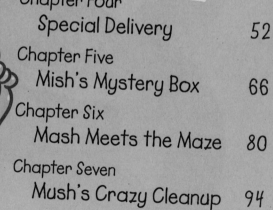

How to use this book

1) Read our hilarious jokes.

2) Laugh, laugh, laugh!

3) Any time you see something
   written on this tape, it's an
   instruction for you to follow.
   Do what it says and you'll be just fine!

I'M AN INSTRUCTION!

CHAPTER ONE

It's a STICKY SITUATION

Why couldn't the cat play on the computer?

Because it kept chasing the mouse!

Yippee!

Let the joke-book building begin!

Where do huskies live?

In the bark-tic!

Knock, knock.
Who's there?
Saturn.
Saturn who?
Saturn a tack and it hurt!

Knock, knock.
Who's there?
Who.
Who who?
Hey, you must be that owl I heard about!

Why didn't the skeleton cross the road?

It didn't have the guts!

Why did the shark brush its teeth?

It wanted to look sharp!

Why did the alien do well in school?

His grades were out of this world!

Why do mother kangaroos hate rainy days?

Because their kids have to play inside.

What's a snake's favorite sport?

Curling.

Where do **mice** keep their boats?

At the hickory-dickory dock.

Where do anteaters like to eat?

What's green and rides on a horse?

Alexander the Grape!

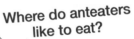

I love hanging up these jokes!

In restaur-ants!

What kind of tree does a **math teacher** climb?

A geoma-tree!

How many magicians does it take to change a **light bulb?**

Only one, but he changed it into a rabbit.

Why did the snake cross the road?

To get to the other sssside.

What animal says doodle-cock-a-doo?

A broken rooster.

You okay over there?

HA! HA!

Why didn't the **pine needle** eat its supper?

Because it was too picky.

What do you call a bear caught in the rain?

A drizzly bear.

What do Martians roast around the campfire?

Martian-mallows!

What time do chickens finish school?

Three o'cluck.

Knock, knock.
Who's there?
Watson.
Watson who?
Watson the back of your truck?

How can you tell an octopus's arms from its legs?

You can't. They're i-tentacle!

What do fish use to call their friends?

Shell phones.

Umm, just having a little bit of trouble...

What kind
of bed does a
**mermaid
sleep in?**

A waterbed.

Why did the
golfer wear two
pairs of pants?

*In case he got
a hole in one!*

Why did the
soccer ball
quit his job?

*He was tired
of being kicked
around!*

How do
cats like
to cook?

*From
scratch!*

What do clouds
wear under
their clothes?

Thunder-wear.

Well, it
looks like you
have things
under control
here.

What do you get
when you cross a
chicken with a
science kit?

An eggs-periment.

I'm going
to get us a
drink.

Why couldn't the
young pirate go
to the movie?

It was rated ARR!

What do you get when you cross a fish with an elephant?

Swimming trunks!

What kind of films do ducks like to watch?

Duck-umentaries.

What's the **noisiest planet?**

Saturn, because it has so many rings!

How do you catch a squirrel?

Climb up a tree and act like a nut!

What did the **ghost** coach say to his ghost players?

Look alive out there!

What food runs in a race?

Fast food.

What do you call a one-eyed monster on wheels?

Cycle-ops!

What is worse than finding a worm in an apple?

Finding half a worm!

Why did the bubblegum cross the road?

Because it was stuck to the chicken's foot.

If bees make honey, what do wasps make?

Wasp-berry jam!

What did one volcano say to the other volcano?

I lava you!

18

What is black-and-white and **sleeps a lot?**

A snooze-paper!

What do you call a kitten drinking lemonade?

A sour-puss!

1 What's small and white and laughs a lot?

2 What do you call a pig that does karate?

A *Because seven ate nine!*

B *Because they are shell-fish!*

3 Why was 6 afraid of 7?

4 Why are crabs so greedy?

Umm... hey! What happened to these jokes?

C *A pork chop.*

D *A tickled onion!*

Answers: 1. D 2. C 3. A 4. B

1 Why did the girl bring a ladder to class?

A *To be with the jelly-fish!*

2 What do you call a rabbit with fleas?

B *A scrap-book!*

3 What's a 10-letter word that starts with gas?

C *When he's coffin!*

ALL the jokes are mixed up! I gotta fix this before Mish comes back!

4 What is the difference between a bird and a fly?

D *The base guitar.*

5 What do you call a disorganized book?

E *Cheer it up!*

20

6

Why did the peanut butter go to sea?

F *Because she was in high school.*

7 What should you do with a blue monster?

G *Bugs bunny!*

8 What musical instrument do baseball players like?

H *The other half!*

9 When is a vampire sick?

I *Automobile.*

10 What looks like half an orange?

J *A bird can fly, but a fly can't bird.*

What do you call a wizard in outer space?

A flying sorcerer.

What do moose read in the morning?

The moose-paper!

When is it hardest to get a ticket to the moon?

When it's full!

What kind of cats go bowling?

Alley cats!

Hey, who wants juice... Huh?! What happened here?

What do elves learn in school?

The elf-abet.

Knock, knock.
Who's there?
Alec.
Alec who?
Alec to go hiking when it's nice out!

What kind of ducks crack jokes?

Wise-quackers!

What do lemons need when they get hurt?

Lemon-aid!

Hi, Mish. Just making sure the jokes don't go anywhere!

What has two wheels and breathes fire?

A dragon riding a bicycle.

Where do you put a noisy dog?

In a barking lot!

CHAPTER TWO

All SHOOK UP

OOOF!

How come I always have to carry the jokes?

What did the boy horse say to the girl **horse?**

Let's prance!

Where would you find a pilot whale?

On board a flying fish!

What's an alien's favorite key on a keyboard?

The space bar.

Knock, knock.
Who's there?
Lettuce.
Lettuce who?
Lettuce in!
It's raining!

What did the **Pacific Ocean** say to the **Atlantic Ocean?**

Nothing, it just waved.

Why don't soccer players eat pizza?

They can't use their hands!

HA! HA!

Hey Mish. Check out this joke!

What goes **"Tick, tick, woof, woof"?**

A watchdog!

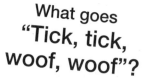

Why do seagulls live near the sea?

If they lived near the bay, they'd be bay-gulls.

Why were the period and the question mark friends?

They had a dot in common!

Why did the boy put lipstick on his head?

To make up his mind!

What can you buy at the dentist for a dollar?

Buck teeth!

What kind of room can't you go into?

A mush-room!

I've got a good one here, too!

Why do scissors make good drivers?

They know all the shortcuts.

What always falls without getting hurt?

Rain.

What did the elephant say when the mouse stepped on its toe?

Pick on somebody your own size.

Why did the student study in an airplane?

He wanted to get higher grades!

Keep those jokes coming, Mash!

How does a book about ducks begin?

With an intro-duck-tion!

Why do seagulls watch the news?

For the feather report!

What sits on your lawn and roars?

A dandy-lion.

Did you hear about the forgetful train conductor?

He lost track of things!

What did the mother bison say to her son when he left for school?

Bye, son!

Why were the teacher's eyes crossed?

He couldn't control his pupils.

What does the sun do when it gets tired?

It sets awhile!

What goes "Ha ha ha ha **plop**"?

Someone laughing her head off!

What's long and orange and wears **diapers**?

A baby carrot.

You bet!

Why was there thunder and lightning at the science fair?

The students were brainstorming!

What happened to the **frog** that sat in a **no-parking** zone?

It got toad away!

Knock, knock.
Who's there?
Phillip.
Phillip who?
Phillip my bag with treats, please!

Do have any more jokes for me, Mash?

Mash?

Where can you find a cheap boat?

$4.99 $2.99 $5.99

At a sail.

What kind of reptile do you find in a hospital?

An ill-igator.

What did one banana say to the other?

Nothing. Bananas can't talk!

30

Why is the shopping so good in Hawaii?

There's isle after isle of savings.

How do you know **mountain climbers** are curious?

Because they are always trying to take another peak!

What has two wings but can't fly?

A hockey team.

WHAT DO THESE SAY?

What is **black-and-white** and **black-and-white**?

A penguin rolling down a hill!

What do you call a polar bear with no socks?

Bear-foot.

Knock, knock.
Who's there?
Iguana.
Iguana who?
Iguana hold your hand!

What kind of parties do trees have?

Lumber parties!

Who is Peter Pan's smelliest friend?

Stinker-bell!

WHAT DO THESE SAY?

Ski jump.

CIRCUS

Three-ring circus.

Where did these come from?

What lives in the desert, has fangs and weighs a lot?

A sumo rattler!

Why did the pine needle do well on the test?

Because he was really sharp!

What do you call a **sleeping bull**?

A bull-dozer.

Why don't bad actors go fishing?

They always forget their lines!

I love to eat chocolate sundaes.

Sandbox.

What's going on?

I ate a pancake today.

Rock star.

Dolphin.

I love to climb trees.

Wagon wheels.

WHOOOAAAA!

WHEEEEHEEHEEHEE!

YEAH! It worked!

CHAPTER THREE

LOOK OUT!

39

What did the balloon say after it **burst?**

Happy burst-day!

Why didn't the dog want to play soccer?

Because it was a boxer.

What's the sweetest dog?

A chocolate lab!

It's one of my favorite jokes. I want to show you, but I can't lift it.

Can you lift it for me?

POSTCODE

SENDER
FROM

POSTCODE

ADDRESSEE

TO

MiSH

HOOOOF!

Whew, that's TOO heavy!

What does Cinderella wear to the beach?

Glass flippers.

What do you call a **ghost on crutches?**

A hobblin' goblin!

Why did the firefly do so well at school?

It was the brightest student!

What's the doctor's favorite musical instrument?

An ear-drum!

What is Tarzan's favorite holiday song?

Jungle Bells!

What did the **banana do** when the **monkey chased it?**

The banana split!

Why did the drum go to bed early?

It was beat!

What kind of plant grows in space?

A sun-flower!

Why should you never tell secrets in a garden?

Because the corn has ears, the potatoes have eyes, and the beans talk.

What do you give to a baby snake?

A rattle!

Thanks for trying, buddy! I've got an idea. I'll be right back...

ADDRESSEE

TO

MiSH

POSTCODE

What do you say to a skeleton going on vacation?

Bone voyage!

What do cows use in math class?

Cow-culators!

How many teeth does a hen have?

None, silly! A hen doesn't have teeth!

Why did the cookie go to the doctor?

Because he felt crumb-y!

What do pigs use to clean the ice rink?

A ham-boni!

What game do mice like to play?

Hide-and-squeak.

What did the wall say to the ceiling?

Meet you at the corner!

What spirit was a great artist?

Vincent Van Ghost.

What do you call a witch who lives in the desert?

A sand-witch!

Hey, what IS this goop?

Why did the **farmer** put bells on his **COWS**?

Because the horns didn't work!

When do astronauts eat their sandwiches?

At launch time.

What do you call a car that can write its own name?

An auto-graph.

What did the snail say when he rode on the turtle's back?

Wheeee!

What is a rabbit's favorite music?

Hip-hop!

What kind of car does **Luke Skywalker** drive?

A To-Yoda!

MiSH

What kind of stone gets lighter the longer you carry it?

A hailstone.

What kind of pants do ghosts wear?

Boo jeans!

What flies but has no wings?

Time.

What's the **same** about a piece of gum and a forest?

They're both stick-y.

What do you call a lion at the North Pole?

Lost!

SUPER gross!

What is wrong with this elephant?

Its feet and legs don't match up.

Which of these shapes is smaller?

They are the same size.

There are lots of small squares inside this big square.

How many can you find altogether?

There are 27 squares.

Which line is longer?

They are the same length.

46

Stare at the bird for 30 seconds, then move your eyes to the cage.

Did you put the bird in the cage?

BLEAAGH!

Do you see a circle or just some straight lines??

WHOA!!

Who is that?

Does line A meet up with line B or C?

Use a ruler to find out.

Which dotted circle is bigger?

They are the same size.

Why did the **cucumber** blush?

He saw the salad dressing!

What bird is a great writer?

A pen-guin!

What do a baby and an old **car have in common?**

They both have a rattle.

What is a vampire's favorite candy?

A sucker!

How do you paint a rabbit's portrait?

With hare-spray!

I'm back! Sorry I took so long!

WHOA!!!

How do you kiss a hockey player?

Pucker up!

ADDRESSEE
TO
MiSH

BANG!

How many triangles do you see?

What do you see? A green vase or two white faces?

What do you see? The inside of a tunnel or the top of a hill?

Mish! Did you see that purple guy?

49

50

Why did the dog stay in the shade?

He didn't want to be a hot dog.

Would Little Miss Muffet share her curds?

No whey!

What kind of table does a math teacher sit at?

A times table.

What do you **say** when a raindrop **falls on your head?**

The sky is falling!

What did the **letter** say to the **envelope?**

Send me.

Why did the boy bring a skunk to school?

For show and smell!

Where does a **snowman keep his money?**

In a snow-bank.

How do billboards talk to each other?

Using sign language.

What did the mom corn say to the baby corn?

Where's your pop corn?

What's green and jumps every five seconds?

A frog with hiccups!

WOO HOO!

I'm a joke-hanging speedster!!

Why are soccer players great at math?

They can use their heads!

What do you call a person who helps out a band?

A Band-aid!

Why is it hard to carry on a conversation with a goat?

Because it's always butting in.

Knock, knock.
Who's there?
P.
P who?
P you. Something stinks.

What does this say?

Bookworm!

What's red and goes up and down?

A tomato in an elevator!

What did the lawn say to the yard?

I've got you covered.

What kind of bug can you measure with?

An inchworm!

Knock, knock.
Who's there?
Ya.
Ya who?
Yahoo! Ride 'em, cowboy!

Why does a tiger have stripes?

So it won't be spotted!

Why was the freshly painted fence so hot?

It had two coats.

What position does a zombie play on a hockey team?

Ghoulie!

What kind of nail does a carpenter not want to hit?

His thumbnail!

What two boys do you always find in school?

Gym and Art!

Why is H the most popular letter?

Because it's at the start of every holiday.

Why did the lifeguard go to the dollar store?

She heard she could save a lot.

BEEEEP! BEEEEEEP!

HEY! Who ordered these boxes?

Who delivers presents to sharks during the holidays?

Santa Jaws.

What did the **polar bear** telephone operator say?

Have an ice day!

Knock, knock.
Who's there?
Turnip.
Turnip who?
Turnip the heat, I'm freezing!

Where do wolves stay when they travel?

At the Howl-iday Inn!

What is a computer's favorite kind of music?

Disc-o!

Where did the monster go when he lost his hand?

The second-hand store!

Mish, MISH! COME QUICK! The purple guy's back!

58

What do ghosts eat for dinner?

Spook-ghetti.

How do you keep a **skunk from smelling?**

Plug its nose.

Knock, knock! Who's there? It's me, Mush. Jokes are boring! This book needs some word puzzles!

WHAT DO THESE SAY?

pig
pig   pig

Three little pigs.

secret ←
secret
secret

Top secret.

HEAD
HEELS

Head over heels.

WHAT DO THESE SAY?
Use a mirror to read the backward messages.
So long to your silly jokes!! My puzzles RULE!
FUTURE FORECASTS FOR FUNNY PHRASES
world
Small world.
JUMPING JAKCS
milli1on
One in a million.
SEE? That's the guy I was talking about!
RAIL ROAD
Railroad crossing.
JUMP
High jump.

What's the best kind of mail to get in the summer?

Fan mail!

Why did the sock cross the road?

Because the chicken was wearing it!

Knock, knock.
Who's there?
Accordian.
Accordian who?
Accordian to my calendar, it's my birthday!

What is a frog's favorite flower?

A croak-us.

What flies but never goes anywhere?

A flag!

What is the perfect age for an eel?

Eel-leven!

Why did the **peanut** go on the spaceship?

It wanted to be an astro-nut!

How do **porcupines** play leapfrog?

Very carefully.

Why did the **football** coach go to the bank?

To get his quarter back!

What has four legs but can't walk?

A table.

What does an **aardvark** like on its pizza?

Ant-chovies.

Where did the purple guy go?

And, what will we do with ALL these boxes?

No worries, Mash! I have an idea.

What's a snake's favorite subject?

Hisss-story!

What do you get when you cross a parrot with a pig?

A bird that hogs the conversation!

What do you call a snowman at a barbecue?

A puddle!

Why do hummingbirds hum?

They don't know the words!

How do tourists greet one another in Hawaii?

Hawaii doing?

HA! HA!

We can use these boxes to carry even MORE JOKES!

Knock, knock.
Who's there?
Boo.
Boo who?
Don't cry, it's only a joke!

What did the tie say to the hat?

You go on a-head and I'll hang around.

What's a bear's favorite card game?

Go fish!

What do spiders do for fun?

Surf the web.

What did the football say to the player?

I get a kick out of you.

Why didn't the piano work?

Because it only knew how to play.

HA! HA!

That's AWESOME!

Why did the **man climb** up a ladder to sing?

So he could reach the high notes!

Why did Jenny get a dog biscuit?

She was the teacher's pet!

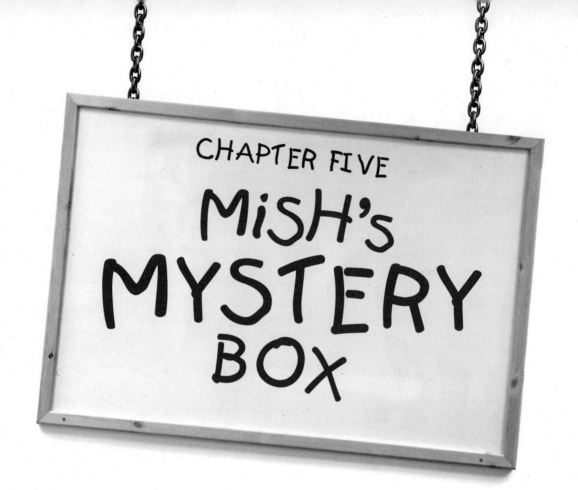

CHAPTER FIVE

MiSH's MYSTERY BOX

67

What is it?

A pig taking a mud bath!

What were **Tarzan's** last words?

Who greased the vine?

How can monkeys fly?

In a hot-air baboon!

What is **at the end** of **everything?**

The letter G.

LOOK!
It's my big box of MAGIC words! They'll make this joke book even better!

What does a mom raccoon have that no other animal has?

Baby raccoons!

Why do giraffes have long necks?

Have you ever smelled their feet?

What's a mummy's favorite musical instrument?

The tomb-ourine!

Why do bookworms like busy hotels?

Because they're all booked up!

What did the tree say to the **lumberjack?**

Leaf me alone!

What can you serve but never eat?

A volleyball.

Huh?!

What's smarter than a talking horse?

A spelling bee!

What did
one octopus say to
the other octopus?

*I want to hold your hand,
hand, hand, hand, hand,
hand, hand, hand.*

What kind of song
can you sing
in space?

A Nep-tune!

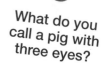

What's a
dog's favorite
movie?

*The Hound
of Music.*

What do you
call a pig with
three eyes?

A piiig.

HA!
HA!

SLIPPERY

Mish, they're
nice words...
but they're NOT
very funny.

Why is a baseball team like a cake?

They both use a batter!

What did the monster truck say to the ant?

I've got a crush on you!

What do baby lobsters sleep in?

Crabs!

How do you hide an elephant in a cherry tree?

You paint its toenails red.

What is a **porcupine's** favorite food?

Prickled onions!

Knock, knock.
Who's there?
Harry.
Harry who?
Harry up or we'll be late!

What is the best way to catch a fish?

Have someone throw it to you!

71

72

Why did the bald man put the rabbit on his head?

He needed the hare.

Why did the apple stay home from school?

It felt rotten!

What has three tails, four trunks and six feet?

An elephant with spare parts!

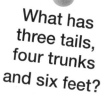

Knock, knock.

Who's there?

Justin.

Justin who?

Justin time for art class!

What did the ballerina wear to math class?

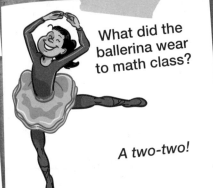

A two-two!

What do you get when you cross a balloon and a teacher?

A pop quiz!

What do you call a **doctor with eight arms?**

A doc-topus!

When a **baker** wants to take a nap, what sign does he **put in the window?**

Do-nut disturb!

How did the artist paint such a nice picture?

Easel-y.

NO MORE JOKES!!!

AAAHHHHH!!!!

What do you call a dentist for vampires?

Brave!

Why did the hairdo get sent to the corner?

It was knotty.

What do spiders like to eat?

French flies!

What kind of ball doesn't bounce?

A snowball.

What kind of Mexican **food** can give you frostbite?

A brrrrr-ito.

What do you get when you stack **toads**?

A toad-em pole!

What did one eye say to the other eye?

Between us, something smells!

Why did the beaver cross the road?

To prove he wasn't chicken!

What do **worms** eat before **supper**?

Apple-tizers.

Hey, Mash! Look what's happening to my MAGIC WORDS!

SLIPPERY SLIDE

SILLY SUSHI

AROUND THE WORLD

AWESOME ALIENS EAT APPLES

MOMMY MADE MARVELOUS MUFFINS

BOUNCING BEACH BALLS

TEN TURTLES TOTTERED TIRELESSLY

FUN IN THE SUN

76

What do **pigs** put on sore toes?

Oink-ment.

What do you get when you cross a border collie with flowers?

Collie-flowers!

What kind of pet lies down and does nothing?

A car-pet!

Who protected the king's castle from being robbed?

Knight watchmen!

Knock, knock.

Who's there?

Hugo.

Hugo who?

Hugo this way and I'll go that way.

What do you get when you cross a **snowman** with a **vampire**?

Frostbite.

Why can't you **tell a joke** to an egg?

It would crack up.

What do trees drink?

Root beer!

How did the egg get up the mountain?

It scrambled!

Who can jump higher than a skyscraper?

Everyone! Skyscrapers can't jump!

What can you put in your right hand but not in your left hand?

Your left elbow.

What do you get when you cross a **parrot with a kitten?**

A copycat!

Knock, knock.

Who's there?

Ivana.

Ivana who?

Ivana come in!

Where does Thursday come before **Wednesday?**

The dictionary!

HEY! I didn't put those riddles up there!

What kind of gum does a bee chew?

Bumble-gum!

Why is the sky so high?

So the birds don't bump their heads.

Why did the gardener plant his money?

He wanted the soil to be rich!

What do dogs eat for breakfast?

Pooched eggs and bark-on!

What ship never sinks?

Friendship!

These riddles are confusing me

OOOH

Knock, knock.
Who's there?
Little old lady.
Little old lady who?
I didn't know you could yodel.

What is round and has two hands?

A clock!

84

What do you get if you cross a centipede with a parrot?

A walkie-talkie!

What do you call a cake that's left in the oven too long?

A burnt-day cake!

Why did the dolphin cross the beach?

To get to the other tide.

What is white, black and green?

A zebra running through a pickle field!

What did the lollipop say to the wrapper?

Stick to me or I'm licked!

Why did the robber take a bath?

He wanted to make a clean getaway!

What goes around the world but stays in a corner?

A stamp!

Perrrfec

Why do fish swim in saltwater?

Because if they swam in pepper, they would sneeze all the time!

What did one worm **say to the other** worm before they ate dinner?

Dig in!

What do trees eat for breakfast?

Root loops!

Knock, knock.
Who's there?
Pasta.
Pasta who?
Pasta gravy, please.

ANSWER THESE RIDDLES

More riddles! Give me MORE riddles!!!

What's at the end of a rainbow?

The letter W.

What has four wheels and flies?

A garbage truck.

Knock, knock.
Who's there?
Howie.
Howie who?
Fine thanks.
Howie you?

What do you get when you cross an elephant with potatoes?

Mashed potatoes!

What goes up and down but doesn't move?

A staircase!

How do you know if there's an **elephant** under your bed?

You bump your nose on the ceiling.

START

I have five eyes, three green ears and a yellow nose. What am I?

Really ugly!

YEAH! My riddles have hypnotized Mash! Now I can put an end to these silly jokes...

...by locking him in my RIDDLE MAZE!!

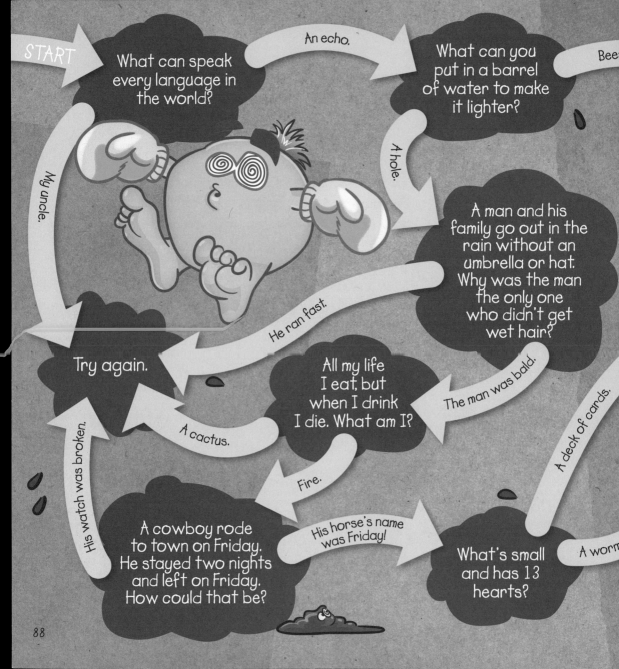

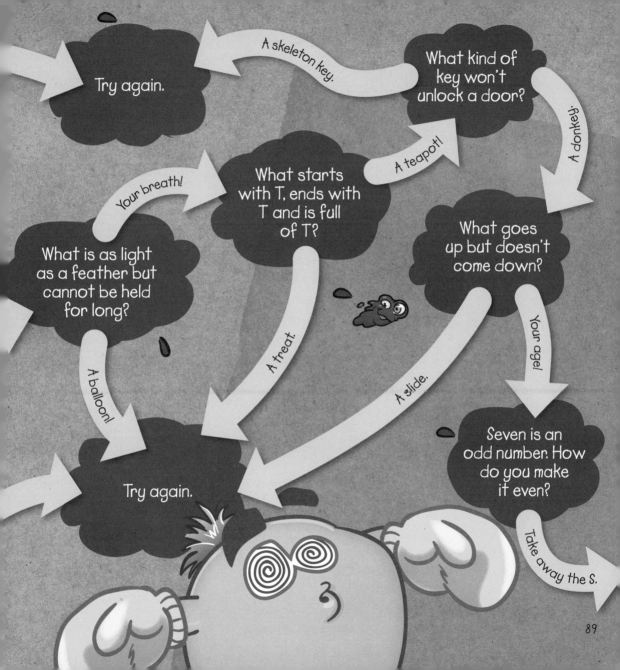

89

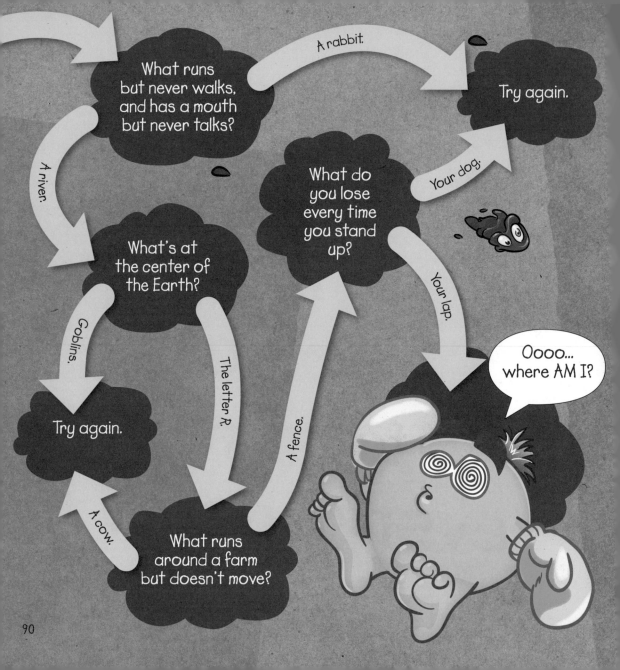

What is **big** and **black** and follows you everywhere?

Your shadow!

CHAPTER SEVEN

MUSH's CRAZY CLEANUP

95

What do you call a mosquito with a tin suit?

A bite in shining armor.

What do you call a train filled with gum?

A chew-chew train!

Where do **cows go** on vacation?

Moo York.

What did the filling say to the donut?

It's jam-packed in here!

What did the number **zero** say to the number **eight?**

Nice belt!

What do you say to a one-year-old frog?

Hoppy birthday!

HA! HA!

Well, all I see now are JOKES everywhere!

YEAH, super-duper silly jokes!!!

How does a dog stop the DVD player?

He hits the paws button!

What do you call an alligator that steers a ship?

A navi-gator!

Knock, knock.
Who's there?
Doris.
Doris who?
Doris locked. That's why I knocked.

What do birds say on Halloween?

Trick or tweet!

What animal can you put in a trance?

A trance-ula.

If a dictionary goes from A to Z, what goes from Z to A?

A zebra.

How do you know carrots are good for your eyesight?

You never see a bunny wearing glasses.

WHHHIRRRRRRRR!!!

97

98

WHHHIRRRRRRRRRR!!!!

Knock, knock.
Who's there?
Rabbit.
Rabbit who?
Rabbit up, it's a birthday present.

What did one rose **say** to the other rose?

How you doing, bud?

What did the dog say after it finished its **dinner?**

Nothing. Dogs can't talk!

Do you think it's hard to spot a leopard?

No, they come that way.

Why did the Egyptian mummy go on vacation?

It needed to unwind!

What kind of vegetables do plumbers like?

Leeks!

What is the best hand to write with? Neither - it's best to write with a pen!

What is the fruitiest subject? History, because it's full of dates!

Knock, knock. Who's there? Abel. Abel who? Abe C D E F G H...

What cheese is made backwards? Edam.

What is a volcano? A mountain with hiccups!

How did the farmer fix his jeans? With a cabbage patch!

Who was the first underwater spy? James Pond!

Why was the broom late? It over-swept!

WHOA!!

What stories do the **ship captain's children** like to hear? Ferry tales!

What pet makes the **loudest noise?** A trum-pet!

What's red and flies and wobbles at the same time? A jelly-copter! Why did the man **take a pencil** to bed? To draw the curtains!

Why did the **dinosaur** cross the **road?** Because chickens weren't invented yet.

101

What kind of horse rides after sunset? A night mare.

What's gray, beautiful and wears glass slippers? Cinder-elephant!

How do snails get their shells so shiny? They use snail polish!

What do you call a gorilla that pots plants? Hairy Potter.

What is white when it's dirty and black when it's clean? A blackboard.

Why do witches ride on brooms? Because vacuums are too heavy.

What do you call an egg spinning through space? A UFO – unidentified frying object!!

102

What kind of bee hums and drops things? A fumble-bee!
What do you get if you cross a frog and a dog? A croaker spaniel!
This is a TIGHT squeeze!
Hmmph! No more jokes for YOU. NOW what will you laugh at?
What did the postcard say to the stamp? Stick with me kid, and we'll go places.

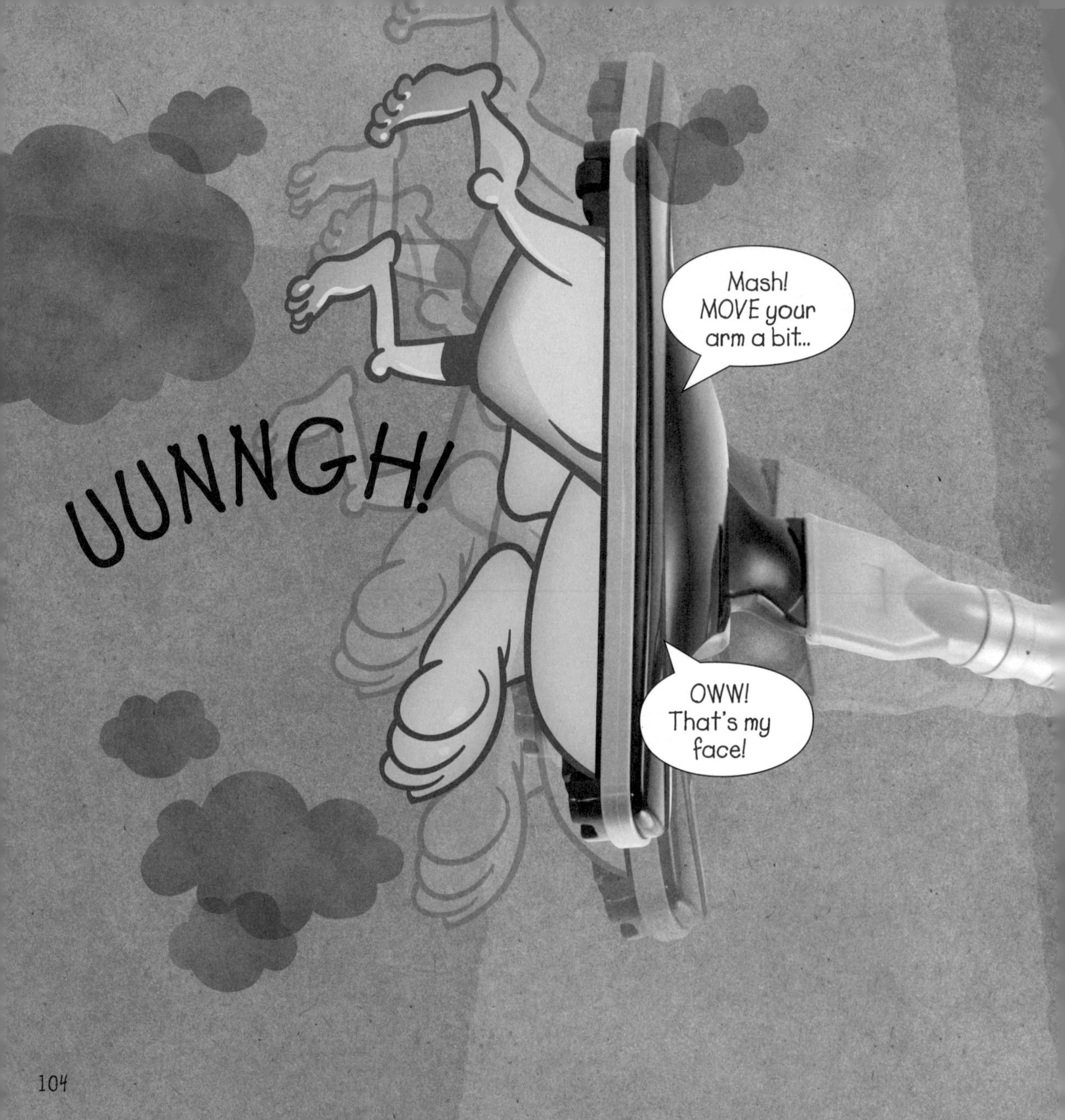
UUNNGH!
Mash! MOVE your arm a bit...
OWW! That's my face!

105

What's the hardest thing about falling out of bed?

The floor.

What are a snowman's two favorite letters?

I.C.

What do you call a dog with **no tail?**

A hot dog!

You need a GOOD LAUGH!!

Why did the Big Dipper eat the moon?

Because it was starving!

What color do books like?

Red!

What medicine do ants take?

Ant-ibiotics.

What did the porcupine say to the cactus in the dark?

Is that you, Mommy?

What's a cat's favorite word?

Purr-fect!

What do you give a sick frog?

A hop-eration!

What's black-and-white and goes around and around?

A dizzy zebra.

HEE HEE

Why didn't Cinderella make the hockey team?

Her coach was a pumpkin!

These ARE pretty funny.

Why didn't the orange finish the race?

It ran out of juice.

What do you get when Godzilla walks through a vegetable garden?

Squash!

What do beavers eat for breakfast?

Oak-meal!

Knock, knock.
Who's there?
Bacon.
Bacon who?
Bacon cookies just for you!

Where do sick insects go?

To the wasp-ital.

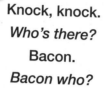

SEE?! You can't resist the power of MY hilarious jokes!

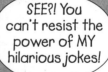

What do you call two banana splits?

A pair of slippers!

112

Where do seals go to watch movies?

To the dive-in!

What kind of cars do rabbits drive?

Hop rods.

Knock, knock.
Who's there?
Sharon.
Sharon who?
Sharon your popcorn with me?

Why didn't the mouse want to go into the lake?

Because there were catfish in the water!

HA! HA!

My jokes are pretty funny, TOO!!

BEEP! BEEP!

What do you call a monkey with firecrackers?

A ba-boom!

113

How do you communicate with a fish?

Drop it a line!

Where did the farmer take his pigs one sunny afternoon?

To a pig-nic!

Why did the boy cry when he was beside the onion?

The onion hurt his peelings!

Why do lions eat their meat raw?

HMMMMMM...

They can't cook!

HA! HA!

These jokes are CRAZY funny!

What do you call a fly with **silver teeth?**

A zipper!

Why isn't there a story about a vampire with a broken tooth?

There's no point to it!

114

What did one teddy bear say to the teddy bear serving dessert?

No, thanks. I'm stuffed!

Why did the student sit on her watch?

She wanted to be on time for class!

Why should you never iron a **four-leaf clover?**

Because you should never press your luck!

Uh, Mish? There's something ELSE that's crazy...

Knock, knock.
Who's there?
Atch.
Atch who?
Bless you!

BEEP!
BEEP!
BEEP!

What do you get when you cross a pig with a centipede?

Bacon and legs.

What do you call 20 rabbits moving backwards?

A receding hare line.

What's green and loud?

A frog-horn.

Looking down at someone's 80th birthday cake.

WHAT'S GOING ON?

COUGH!

MUSH!! That's what's going on!

COUGH!

116

Four raisins skipping rope.

An armchair.

A starfish.

GRRR!!

117

WHAT IS IT?
Square dancing.
A snake chasing its own tail.
At first, you see a cat. Turn it sideways and you see a pointing finger.
Frankenstein in front of you at the movies.
COUGH!
Hey, these puzzles ARE kinda funny!
YEAH! They are!

A snowman in July.

A rainbow.

A UFO chasing a giant egg.

They're REALLY funny!

HA! HA!

HA! HA! HA!

120

CHAPTER NINE

RiDiNG THE WAVE

123

Where do ghosts like to swim?

Lake Eerie!

Knock, knock.
Who's there?
Annie.
Annie who?
Annie-body home?

How do you make a milkshake?

Sneak up behind it and say "Boo!"

What part of the fish weighs the most?

The scales!

I LOVE jokes, too! But maybe this book needs something else.

How does a mother Dalmatian find her kids?

She spots them!

What did the **apple tree** say to the **farmer?**

Stop picking on me!

What do **mermaids use for money?**

Sand dollars.

Knock, knock.
Who's there?
Luke.
Luke who?
Luke through the keyhole and see!

What kind of cars do boxers drive?

Punch buggies!

WHAT? Something else? But jokes are SO funny!

HA! HA!

Where do pilots drink their soda pop?

In the coke-pit!

How do hikers cross a patch of poison ivy?

They itch-hike.

Where do **Martians** leave their spaceships?

At parking meteors!

What has a neck but no head and wears a cap?

A bottle!

What lives underwater and carries a lot of people?

An octo-bus!

Oh, NO!! More purple goop!

What did the toilet paper say when it got torn?

What a rip-off!

What do you call a woman with a sheep on her head?

Baa-baa-ra!

YIKES, Mush is back!

How do bees get to school?

The school buzz!

Why did the boy throw the butter out the window?

He wanted to see the butter fly!

What do you get if you cross an elephant and a kangaroo?

Big holes all over Australia!

What do you get when you cross a clown with a mountain goat?

A silly billy!

Knock, knock.
Who's there?
Sid.
Sid who?
Sid down and have an iced tea.

What did one math book say to the other?

Have any problems?

Which hand should you use to pick up a snake?

Someone else's!

What has four wheels and roars down the highway?

A lion on a skateboard!

What kind of pet does a spy have?

A spy-der!

Where do **COWS** stay on **vacation?**

At a moo-tel.

What did one toilet say to the other toilet?

You look a bit flushed!

It's a flood of GROSS GOOP!

HEY! I have an idea. Let's go swimming!

HA!
HA!

How did the carpenter break his tooth?

He chewed his nails!

I'm going to wash ALL the jokes out of your silly book!!!

Why did the traffic light turn **red**?

It was embarrassed to have to change in front of everyone!

What **game** do fish **like** to play?

Salmon says!

Knock, knock.
Who's there?
Colin.
Colin who?
Colin the doctor.
I don't feel well.

Knock, knock.
Who's there?
Art.
Art who?
Art you going to let me in?

Why are vampire movies on late at night?

Because they can't be in the sun!

WHEEE!

This is a BLAST! And we can always find more jokes!

What do you call a man who goes **fishing** all day? *Rod!*

When are there 24 letters in the **alphabet**? *When U and I run away!*

Why did the hot dog put on a sweater?

Because he was a chili dog!

What kind of reptile is always on the phone?

A croco-dial!

What do **elves** like to eat?

Elf-alfa sprouts.

HA! HA!

YEAH! This IS fun!

What is the best thing to put in your **dessert**? *Your teeth!*

What is a **chicken's** favorite plant? *An egg-plant!*

What time is it when two bears chase you? *Two after one!*

What bird can lift the heaviest weights?

The crane!

WHEEEE-HEE-HEE-HEE!

What kind of shirts do turtles wear? Turtlenecks, of course!

Where do cows go to look at art? The moo-seum.

What do you say after you get off a boat? Thank you ferry much!

Why do astronauts like to take off? Because it's a blast!

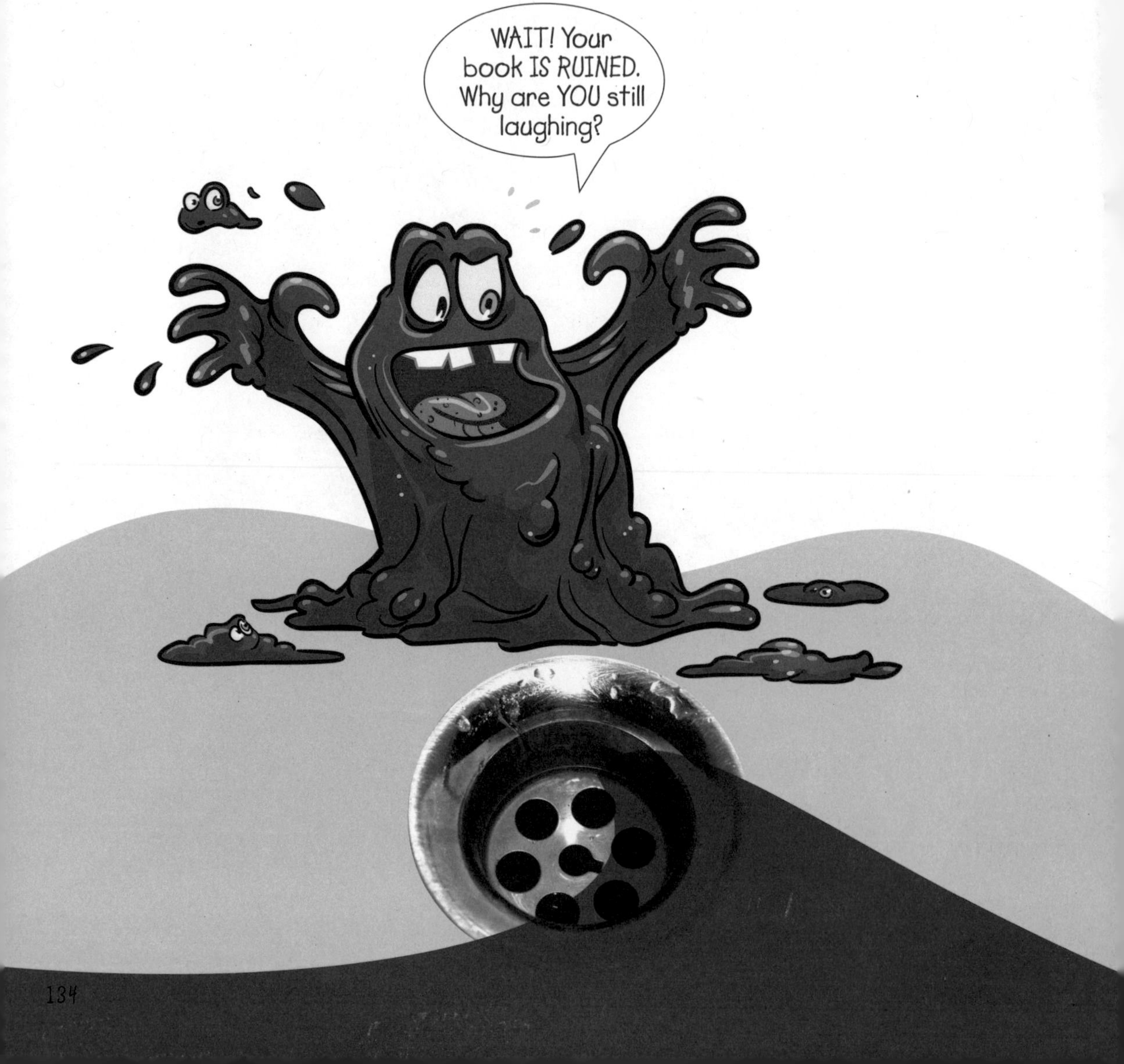
WAIT! Your book IS RUINED. Why are YOU still laughing?

135

CHAPTER TEN

THE PERFECT JOKE BOOK!

Why did the firefly do so well in the race?

He was all fired up!

What do you call an ant that is good at math?

An account-ant!

What did the **judge say** when the **skunk** went into the courtroom?

Odor in the court.

We have WACKY jokes...

Knock, knock.
Who's there?
Colleen.
Colleen who?
Colleen this house.
It's a mess!

Why wouldn't they let the butterfly into the dance?

Because it was a moth ball.

Why do lumberjacks like computers?

Because they get to log on!

What do the police use to patrol the seashore?

A squid car!

Which is faster, hot or cold?

Hot! You can catch cold!

...and even MORE wacky jokes!

Why was the ocean embarrassed?

Because everyone could see its bottom!

Knock, knock.
Who's there?
Cargo.
Cargo who?
Car go "beep-beep"!

What do you call a deer that can't see?

No eye deer!

139

What do you call
a happy mushroom?

A fun-guy!

Why did the student
eat his homework?

*Because the
teacher said it was
a piece of cake!*

What's worse
than raining
cats and dogs?

Hailing taxis.

What is the difference
between here and there?

The letter T!

But even
better, NOW
we've got...

What do you get
if you cross
a sheep and a
porcupine?

*An animal that knits its
own sweaters.*

What is the best way to talk to a monster?

Long distance!

If you drop a **white hat** into the **Red Sea,** what does it become?

Wet.

Why did the farmer buy a brown cow?

Because he wanted chocolate milk.

What do you get when you cross a baseball player and a fork?

A pitchfork!

What gets wetter the more it dries?

A towel.

...RIDDLES!

Who serves **ice cream** faster than a **speeding bullet?**

Scooperman!

What did the bee say when he saw the honeycomb?

Comb, sweet comb!

What do you give a horse with a cold?

Cough stirrup!

JIGGLY JUMPING JELLY

What book tells you all about **chickens?**

A hen-cyclopedia.

...and SILLY SKETCHES!

...and BRAIN-BENDING word puzzles!

Worm's-eye view of four hungry birds.

Class clown.

142

What do you call a snake on a car window?

A windshield viper!

Use a mirror to read the backward messages.

WAILING WHALES WANT WHEAT WAFERS

Why did the **scientist** install a **knocker** on his door?

He wanted to win the no-bell prize!

...and, umm, OPTICAL ILLUSIONS?

Stare at the dot for one minute then look up. What do you see?

How many full cubes can you count in this pattern. Six or seven?

BROTHER

Big brother.

143

What animal is hard to play cards with?

A cheetah!

A skier who crashed into a tree.

When is a crayon sad?

When it's blue!

It's MEGA-fun!

YEAH! It's a DOOZY of a joke book!

cheese

Blue cheese.

Butterfly.

What starts with E, ends with E but usually has one letter?

An envelope.

Is the middle prong attached??

Which way are these stairs headed? Up or down?

What do whales eat?

Fish and ships!

A shark with a pierced fin.

A giraffe passing by a window.

Hey! Do you REALLY like my puzzles?

WIN WITH WACKY WORDS

145

Why did Dracula fail art class?

He only drew blood.

The more of these you take, the more you leave behind. What are they?

Footsteps.

A man looking down a manhole cover.

What do you see? A lady or a musician? Or both?

Where do pencils come from?

Pencil-vania!

RAINING RUBBER RUBIES

I LOVE your puzzles, Mush! They're JUST what this joke book needs!

What did the cat say to the mouse?

Pleased to eat you.

What do you call a town in space?

A com-moon-ity!

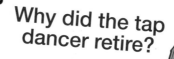

CUTE
CATS
CATCH
COMMON
COLDS

Gee, thanks!

Why did the tap dancer retire?

He kept falling in the sink.

W
WALK
L
K

Crosswalk.

See guys, we made the PERFECT joke book!!

147

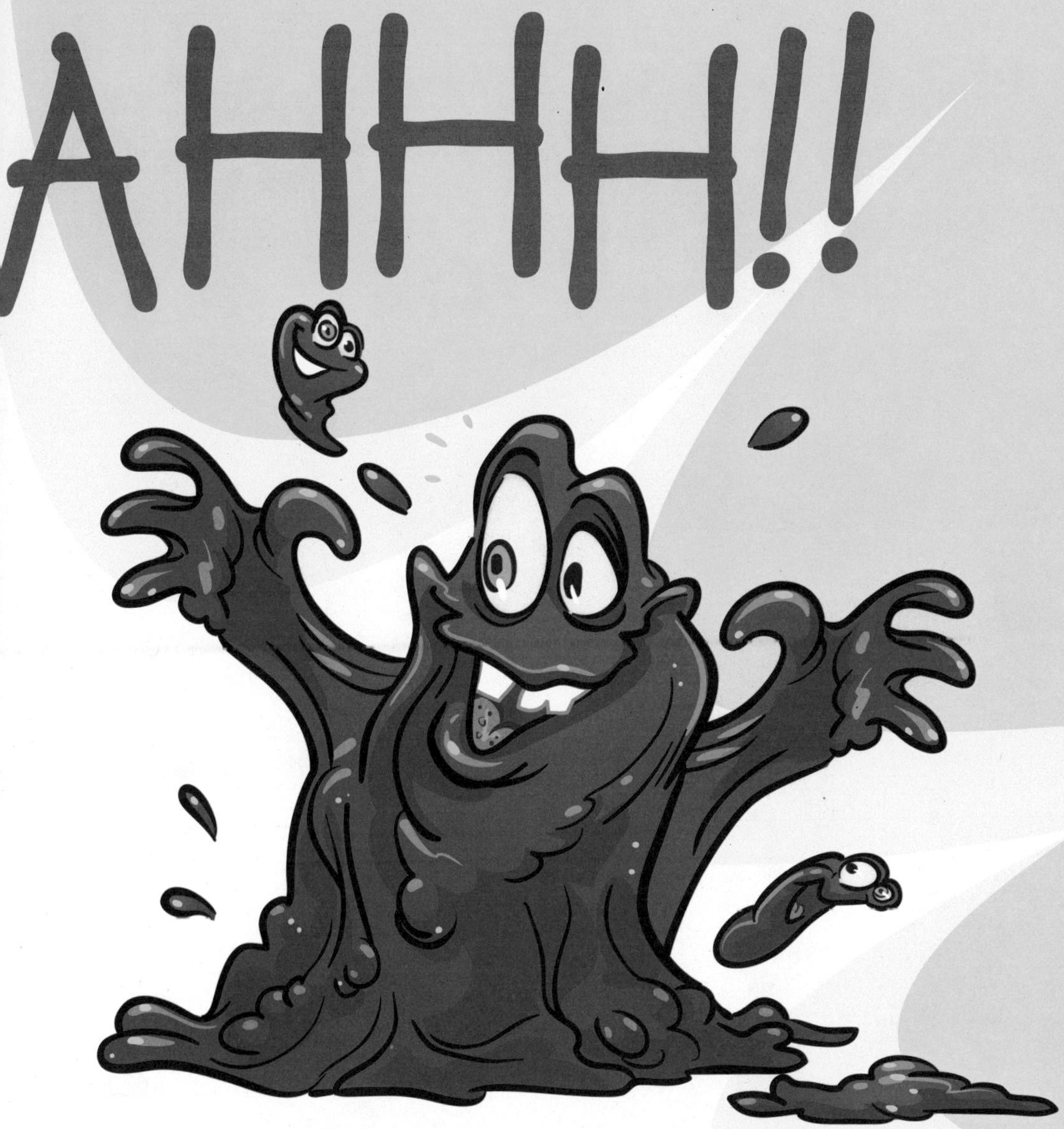
AHHH!!

Now YOU can learn how to draw us yourself!

Mish

Draw the letter M for the tongue.

Mash

His hair looks like the top of a hairbrush.

150

HOW TO DRAW MISH

Mish is one smart monster. The only thing he likes more than making crazy plans is laughing at hilarious jokes. Mish thinks he and his buddy Mash can do anything if they just try.

Favorite saying:
Aha! I've got an idea!

Favorite snack:
Green socks and melted ice cream.

Special trick:
Floats on his back when he sleeps.

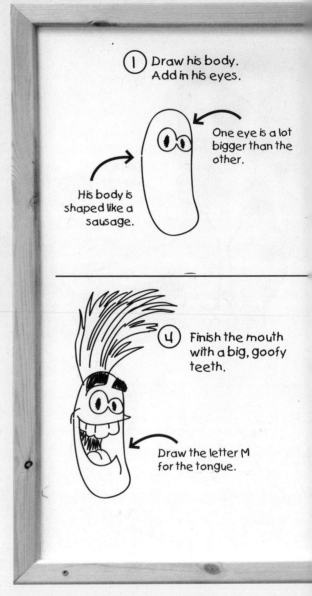

1 Draw his body. Add in his eyes.

One eye is a lot bigger than the other.

His body is shaped like a sausage.

4 Finish the mouth with a big, goofy teeth.

Draw the letter M for the tongue.

152

② Add his eyebrows and mouth.

His eyebrows can pop off his face a little.

③ Add the long, spiky hair.

It looks like a big, tall ocean wave.

⑤ Draw circles for hands and sausages for feet!

Connect them to his body by drawing two lines.

⑥ Draw in his three fingers and thumb.

Add a circle to make his knobby elbows and knees.

Mash looks up to Mish and will do anything to lend his friend a hand. He's super-strong but also a little clumsy. He always wears giant mittens. Mish tells him they look cool.

Favorite saying:
I, uh, didn't, uh, mean to do that.

Favorite snack:
Boulder mud cakes.

Special trick:
Can bowl ten perfect games in a row while blindfolded.

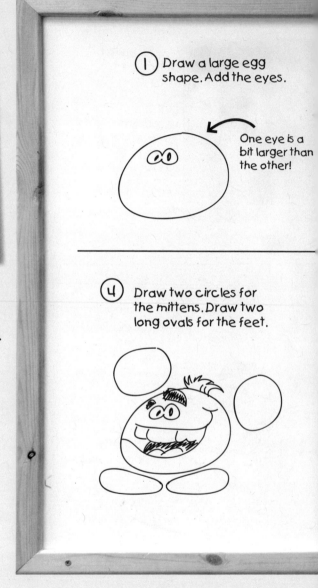

1 Draw a large egg shape. Add the eyes.

One eye is a bit larger than the other!

4 Draw two circles for the mittens. Draw two long ovals for the feet.

154

② Add big, thick eyebrows.
Draw three lines to make the mouth.

They're rounded rectangles

③ Add a short patch of hair.
Finish the mouth with big teeth.

It looks like the top of a hairbrush.

Draw the letter M for the tongue.

⑤ Draw in thumbs on the mittens. Draw rectangles under the circles to complete the mittens.

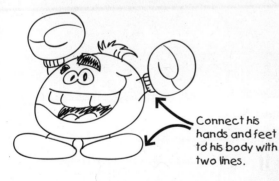

Connect his hands and feet to his body with two lines.

⑥ Draw a big C followed by three connecting small letter C's for his toes.

Draw backwards C's on his other foot.

Mush thinks that jokes are a waste of time, and that Mish and Mash need to be taught a lesson. He doesn't like to laugh very much. In fact, the only things he does like are puzzles, riddles and optical illusions.

Favorite saying:
Blech!

Favorite snack:
Spinach soup with sardines on dried beetle toast.

Special trick:
Creates little creatures when he leaves a trail of goo.

① Draw a big, blobby mess.

④ To add a hand, draw an oval. Connect his hand to his body with two lines.

Mush doesn't always have arms but they pop out when he needs them.

② Draw one big eye and one small eye.

Add a small black dot.

Make a circle with a little black dot.

③ Add a mouth by making a wavy line.

⑤ Add jagged, square lines for teeth and the letter M to make a tongue.

Add ovals to make fingers

⑥ Try drawing blobs with funny faces.

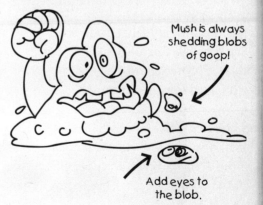

Mush is always shedding blobs of goop!

Add eyes to the blob.

Remie Geoffroi illustrates the popular "Mish Mash" page each month in *chickaDEE Magazine*. Before becoming a full-time freelance illustrator, he worked at an animation studio, a T-shirt company, the Canadian Museum of Civilization and the *National Post*.

In addition to his coast-to-coast Canadian travels, he has crossed the globe, from Indonesia and Australia (where he pet kangaroos and koalas, visited the Sydney Opera House) to India (visited the Taj Mahal, rode an elephant through the jungle!), the Caribbean, Polynesia and Europe, where he lived for a few months.

When he's not drawing Mish, Mash and Mush, you can find Remie strolling beside the Ottawa River with his wife, Chrystal, and baby, Gabriel, or playing with his cat, Shazam!

When I draw Mish, Mash and Mush I sketch in light-blue pencil crayon, and then trace over the best lines with a darker color.